THIS BOOK BELONGS TO

_____

WANT FREE GOODIES?!

Email us at

prettysimplebooks@gmail.com

Title the email "Today is the Day!"
and let us know that you purchased
a Food + Fitness Journal and we'll
send you something fun!

Questions & Customer Service:
Email us at prettysimplebooks@gmail.com!

GET YOUR Goals ON PAPER

GOAL . . . .

NUTRITION

_____

_____

_____

_____

EXERCISE

_____

_____

_____

_____

HYDRATION

_____

_____

_____

_____

SLEEP

_____

_____

_____

_____

WHAT'S YOUR Why

Take a minute to jot some thoughts down on paper. What's your WHY? What is your motivation? This is the page you'll come back to when you need a reminder of why you are choosing to put your body and your health first.

_____
_____
_____
_____
_____
_____
_____
_____
_____
_____
_____
_____
_____
_____
_____
_____
_____
_____
_____
_____
_____
_____

THE STARTING POINT

STATS

WEIGHT ....

CHEST ....

WAIST ....

HIPS ....

THIGH ....

CALF ....

OVERALL FEELINGS TOWARDS:

NUTRITION

TERRIBLE   NOT GOOD   I'M OKAY   GRRREAT   FOOD NINJA

EXERCISE

TERRIBLE   NOT GOOD   I'M OKAY   GRRREAT   EXERCISE NINJA

YOU ARE
Awesome

GO GET 'EM!

DATE _____

TODODAY I ATE..

BREAKFAST

_____

_____

_____

_____

LUNCH

_____

_____

_____

_____

DINNER

_____

_____

_____

_____

—— SNACKS ——

_____

WATER INTAKE ▽▽▽▽▽▽▽▽ ___ TOTAL OZ.

EXERCISE..

_____

_____

_____

_____

I HAD: ☐ AN AWESOME DAY! ☐ I CAN DO BETTER!

DATE _____

. . . . I SLEPT ___ HOURS LAST NIGHT. . . . . . .

TODAY I ATE...

BREAKFAST

_____
_____
_____
_____

LUNCH

_____
_____
_____
_____

DINNER

_____
_____
_____
_____

——— SNACKS ———

WATER INTAKE ▽▽▽▽▽▽▽ ___ TOTAL OZ.

EXERCISE...

_____
_____
_____
_____

I HAD: ☐ AN AWESOME DAY! ☐ I CAN DO BETTER!

DATE _____

I SLEPT ____ HOURS LAST NIGHT.

TODAY I ATE...

BREAKFAST

_____

_____

_____

LUNCH

_____

_____

_____

DINNER

_____

_____

_____

—— SNACKS ——

_____

WATER INTAKE ⬜⬜⬜⬜⬜⬜⬜ _____ TOTAL OZ.

EXERCISE...

_____

_____

_____

_____

I HAD: ☐ AN AWESOME DAY! ☐ I CAN DO BETTER!

DATE _____

· · · · · · · I SLEPT ___ HOURS LAST NIGHT. · · · · · ·

TODAY I ATE...

BREAKFAST

_____
_____
_____   — SNACKS —
_____

LUNCH

_____
_____
_____
_____

DINNER

_____
_____
_____   _____
_____

WATER INTAKE ▽▽▽▽▽▽▽▽ ___ TOTAL OZ.

EXERCISE...

_____
_____
_____
_____
_____

I HAD: ☐ AN AWESOME DAY! ☐ I CAN DO BETTER!

DATE _____

· · · · · · · · **I SLEPT ___ HOURS LAST NIGHT.** · · · · · · ·

TODAY I ATE...

BREAKFAST

_____

_____

_____

_____

LUNCH

_____

_____

_____

_____

DINNER

_____

_____

_____

_____

—— SNACKS ——

_____

WATER INTAKE ⛉⛉⛉⛉⛉⛉⛉⛉ _____ TOTAL OZ.

EXERCISE..

_____

_____

_____

_____

_____

I HAD: ☐ AN AWESOME DAY! ☐ I CAN DO BETTER!

DATE _____

. . . . **I SLEPT____ HOURS LAST NIGHT.** . . . .

TODAY I ATE..

BREAKFAST

_____
_____
_____   ┌─── SNACKS ───┐
_____

LUNCH

_____
_____
_____
_____

DINNER

_____
_____
_____   └_____┘

WATER INTAKE ▽▽▽▽▽▽▽ ____ TOTAL OZ.

EXERCISE..

_____
_____
_____
_____

I HAD: ☐ AN AWESOME DAY! ☐ I CAN DO BETTER!

DATE _____

TODAY I ATE..

BREAKFAST

_____

_____

_____

LUNCH

_____

_____

_____

DINNER

_____

_____

_____

— SNACKS —

_____

WATER INTAKE ▽▽▽▽▽▽▽▽ _____ TOTAL OZ.

EXERCISE...

_____

_____

_____

_____

I HAD: ☐ AN AWESOME DAY! ☐ I CAN DO BETTER!

DATE _____

TODAY I ATE..

BREAKFAST

_____
_____
_____
_____

LUNCH

_____
_____
_____
_____

DINNER

_____
_____
_____
_____

—— SNACKS ——

WATER INTAKE ⊔⊔⊔⊔⊔⊔⊔⊔ ____ TOTAL OZ.

EXERCISE...

_____
_____
_____
_____

I HAD: ☐ AN AWESOME DAY! ☐ I CAN DO BETTER!

DATE _____

. . . . I SLEPT ___ HOURS LAST NIGHT. . . . .

TODAY I ATE..

BREAKFAST
_____
_____
_____
_____

LUNCH
_____
_____
_____
_____

DINNER
_____
_____
_____
_____

——— SNACKS ———

_____

WATER INTAKE ▽▽▽▽▽▽▽▽ _____ TOTAL OZ.

EXERCISE...

_____
_____
_____
_____

I HAD: ☐ AN AWESOME DAY! ☐ I CAN DO BETTER!

DATE _____

• • • • • • • I SLEPT____ HOURS LAST NIGHT. • • • • • • •

TODAY I ATE...

BREAKFAST

_____
_____
_____
_____

LUNCH

_____
_____
_____
_____

DINNER

_____
_____
_____
_____

—— SNACKS ——

_____

WATER INTAKE 〇〇〇〇〇〇〇 ____ TOTAL OZ.

EXERCISE...

_____
_____
_____
_____

I HAD: ☐ AN AWESOME DAY! ☐ I CAN DO BETTER!

DATE _____

| . . . . I SLEPT ___ HOURS LAST NIGHT. . . . . . . |

TODY I ATE...

BREAKFAST

_____
_____
_____
_____

LUNCH

_____
_____
_____
_____

DINNER

_____
_____
_____
_____

——— SNACKS ———

_____

WATER INTAKE ⏣⏣⏣⏣⏣⏣⏣⏣ ____ TOTAL OZ.

EXERCISE...

_____
_____
_____
_____

I HAD: ☐ AN AWESOME DAY! ☐ I CAN DO BETTER!

DATE _____

• • • • • • I SLEPT___ HOURS LAST NIGHT. • • • • • •

TODAY I ATE...

BREAKFAST

_____

_____

_____

LUNCH

_____

_____

_____

DINNER

_____

_____

_____

— SNACKS —

WATER INTAKE ⊔⊔⊔⊔⊔⊔⊔ ___ TOTAL OZ.

EXERCISE..

_____

_____

_____

_____

I HAD: ☐ AN AWESOME DAY! ☐ I CAN DO BETTER!

DATE _____

TODAY I ATE...

BREAKFAST

_____
_____
_____
_____

LUNCH

_____
_____
_____
_____

DINNER

_____
_____
_____
_____

——— SNACKS ———

_____

WATER INTAKE ⊔⊔⊔⊔⊔⊔⊔ ___ TOTAL OZ.

EXERCISE...

_____
_____
_____
_____

I HAD: ☐ AN AWESOME DAY! ☐ I CAN DO BETTER!

Just Start

DATE _____

TODAY I ATE...

BREAKFAST

_____
_____
_____
_____

LUNCH

_____
_____
_____
_____

DINNER

_____
_____
_____
_____

—— SNACKS ——

_____

WATER INTAKE ⊔⊔⊔⊔⊔⊔⊔ —— TOTAL OZ.

EXERCISE..

_____
_____
_____
_____

I HAD: ☐ AN AWESOME DAY! ☐ I CAN DO BETTER!

DATE _____

I SLEPT ___ HOURS LAST NIGHT.

TODAY I ATE..

BREAKFAST

_____
_____
_____

— SNACKS —

LUNCH

_____
_____
_____
_____

DINNER

_____
_____
_____
_____

WATER INTAKE ⏣⏣⏣⏣⏣⏣⏣ ___ TOTAL OZ.

EXERCISE...

_____
_____
_____
_____

I HAD: ☐ AN AWESOME DAY! ☐ I CAN DO BETTER!

DATE _____

> • • • • • • • **I SLEPT____ HOURS LAST NIGHT.** • • • • • •

TODAY I ATE...

BREAKFAST

_____
_____
_____
_____

LUNCH

_____
_____
_____
_____

DINNER

_____
_____
_____
_____

──── SNACKS ────

_____

WATER INTAKE ▽▽▽▽▽▽▽▽ _____ TOTAL OZ.

EXERCISE..

_____
_____
_____
_____

I HAD: ☐ AN AWESOME DAY! ☐ I CAN DO BETTER!

DATE _____

• • • • • • • I SLEPT ___ HOURS LAST NIGHT. • • • • • •

TODAY I ATE...

BREAKFAST
_____
_____
_____

LUNCH
_____
_____
_____

DINNER
_____
_____
_____

—— SNACKS ——
_____

WATER INTAKE ⛶⛶⛶⛶⛶⛶⛶ ___ TOTAL OZ.

EXERCISE...
_____
_____
_____
_____

I HAD: ☐ AN AWESOME DAY! ☐ I CAN DO BETTER!

DATE _____

. . . . I SLEPT ___ HOURS LAST NIGHT. . . . .

TODAY I ATE..

BREAKFAST

_____

_____

_____   ——— SNACKS ———

_____

LUNCH

_____

_____

_____

_____

DINNER

_____

_____

_____   _____

WATER INTAKE ⛃⛃⛃⛃⛃⛃⛃ _____ TOTAL OZ.

EXERCISE...

_____

_____

_____

_____

I HAD: ☐ AN AWESOME DAY! ☐ I CAN DO BETTER!

DATE _____

. . . . **I SLEPT___ HOURS LAST NIGHT.** . . . . . .

TODAY I ATE..

BREAKFAST

_____

_____

_____

LUNCH

_____

_____

_____

DINNER

_____

_____

_____

—— SNACKS ——

WATER INTAKE ⊔⊔⊔⊔⊔⊔⊔ ___ TOTAL OZ.

EXERCISE..

_____

_____

_____

_____

I HAD: ☐ AN AWESOME DAY! ☐ I CAN DO BETTER!

DATE _____

. . . . **I SLEPT ___ HOURS LAST NIGHT.** . . . .

TODEY I ATE...

BREAKFAST

_____

_____

_____

_____

LUNCH

_____

_____

_____

DINNER

_____

_____

_____

_____

— SNACKS —

_____

WATER INTAKE ⑁⑁⑁⑁⑁⑁⑁⑁ ____ TOTAL OZ.

EXERCISE...

_____

_____

_____

_____

I HAD: ☐ AN AWESOME DAY! ☐ I CAN DO BETTER!

DATE _____

• • • • • • • **I SLEPT** ___ **HOURS LAST NIGHT.** • • • • • • •

TODAY I ATE..

BREAKFAST

_____
_____
_____
_____

LUNCH

_____
_____
_____
_____

DINNER

_____
_____
_____
_____

— SNACKS —

_____

WATER INTAKE ⛉⛉⛉⛉⛉⛉⛉ ___ TOTAL OZ.

EXERCISE...

_____
_____
_____
_____

I HAD: ☐ AN AWESOME DAY! ☐ I CAN DO BETTER!

DATE _____

. . . . **I SLEPT ___ HOURS LAST NIGHT.** . . . . . .

TODAY I ATE..

BREAKFAST

_____
_____
_____
_____

—— SNACKS ——

LUNCH

_____
_____
_____

DINNER

_____
_____
_____
_____

_____

WATER INTAKE ⛶⛶⛶⛶⛶⛶⛶⛶ ___ TOTAL OZ.

EXERCISE...

_____
_____
_____
_____

I HAD: ☐ AN AWESOME DAY! ☐ I CAN DO BETTER!

DATE _____

I SLEPT ___ HOURS LAST NIGHT.

TODAY I ATE...

BREAKFAST

_____

_____

_____

LUNCH

_____

_____

_____

DINNER

_____

_____

_____

——— SNACKS ———

WATER INTAKE ⊔⊔⊔⊔⊔⊔⊔ ____ TOTAL OZ.

EXERCISE...

_____

_____

_____

_____

I HAD: ☐ AN AWESOME DAY! ☐ I CAN DO BETTER!

DATE _____

· · · · · · · · I SLEPT__ HOURS LAST NIGHT. · · · · · · ·

TODAY I ATE..

BREAKFAST

_____

_____

_____

_____

LUNCH

_____

_____

_____

_____

DINNER

_____

_____

_____

_____

—— SNACKS ——

_____

WATER INTAKE ⛶⛶⛶⛶⛶⛶⛶⛶ ___ TOTAL OZ.

EXERCISE..

_____

_____

_____

_____

I HAD: ☐ AN AWESOME DAY! ☐ I CAN DO BETTER!

DATE _____

• • • • • • • I SLEPT___ HOURS LAST NIGHT. • • • • • • •

TODAY I ATE...

BREAKFAST

_____

_____

_____

LUNCH

_____

_____

_____

DINNER

_____

_____

_____

—— SNACKS ——

WATER INTAKE ▽▽▽▽▽▽▽▽ ___ TOTAL OZ.

EXERCISE ....

_____

_____

_____

_____

I HAD: ☐ AN AWESOME DAY! ☐ I CAN DO BETTER!

DATE _____

TODAY I ATE..

BREAKFAST

_____

_____

_____

_____

LUNCH

_____

_____

_____

DINNER

_____

_____

_____

_____

—— SNACKS ——

_____

WATER INTAKE ▽▽▽▽▽▽▽ ___ TOTAL OZ.

EXERCISE..

_____

_____

_____

_____

I HAD: ☐ AN AWESOME DAY! ☐ I CAN DO BETTER!

YOU ARE STRONGER THAN YOU THINK

DATE _____

· · · · · · · I SLEPT ___ HOURS LAST NIGHT. · · · · · ·

TODAY I ATE...

BREAKFAST

_____
_____
_____

LUNCH

_____
_____
_____
_____

DINNER

_____
_____
_____
_____

—— SNACKS ——

_____

WATER INTAKE ⛛⛛⛛⛛⛛⛛⛛⛛ ____ TOTAL OZ.

EXERCISE...

_____
_____
_____
_____

I HAD: ☐ AN AWESOME DAY! ☐ I CAN DO BETTER!

DATE _____

· · · · · · · I SLEPT ___ HOURS LAST NIGHT. · · · · · ·

TODAY I ATE...

BREAKFAST

_____
_____
_____

LUNCH

_____
_____
_____

DINNER

_____
_____
_____

—— SNACKS ——

_____

WATER INTAKE ⬜⬜⬜⬜⬜⬜⬜⬜ ___ TOTAL OZ.

EXERCISE...

_____
_____
_____
_____

I HAD: ☐ AN AWESOME DAY! ☐ I CAN DO BETTER!

DATE _____

· · · · · · · I SLEPT ___ HOURS LAST NIGHT. · · · · · · ·

TODAY I ATE...

BREAKFAST

_____

_____

_____   —— SNACKS ——

LUNCH

_____

_____

_____

DINNER

_____

_____   _____

_____

WATER INTAKE ▽▽▽▽▽▽▽ _____ TOTAL OZ.

EXERCISE...

_____

_____

_____

_____

I HAD: ☐ AN AWESOME DAY! ☐ I CAN DO BETTER!

DATE _____

I SLEPT ___ HOURS LAST NIGHT.

TODAY I ATE...

BREAKFAST

_____
_____
_____

LUNCH

_____
_____
_____

DINNER

_____
_____
_____

SNACKS

WATER INTAKE ⊔⊔⊔⊔⊔⊔⊔ ___ TOTAL OZ.

EXERCISE...

_____
_____
_____
_____

I HAD: ☐ AN AWESOME DAY! ☐ I CAN DO BETTER!

DATE _____

· · · · · · · I SLEPT ___ HOURS LAST NIGHT. · · · · · · ·

TODAY I ATE..

BREAKFAST
_____
_____
_____
_____

LUNCH
_____
_____
_____
_____

DINNER
_____
_____
_____
_____

—— SNACKS ——

_____

WATER INTAKE ⊽⊽⊽⊽⊽⊽⊽⊽ ___ TOTAL OZ.

EXERCISE...

_____
_____
_____
_____

I HAD: ☐ AN AWESOME DAY! ☐ I CAN DO BETTER!

DATE _____

. . . . I SLEPT___ HOURS LAST NIGHT. . . . . . .

TODAY I ATE...

BREAKFAST

_____
_____
_____

LUNCH

_____
_____
_____

DINNER

_____
_____
_____

—— SNACKS ——

_____

WATER INTAKE ⛢⛢⛢⛢⛢⛢⛢⛢ ___ TOTAL OZ.

EXERCISE..

_____
_____
_____
_____

I HAD: ☐ AN AWESOME DAY! ☐ I CAN DO BETTER!

DATE _____

· · · · · · · **I SLEPT___ HOURS LAST NIGHT.** · · · · · ·

TODAY I ATE. . . . .

BREAKFAST

_____

_____

_____

LUNCH

_____

_____

_____

DINNER

_____

_____

_____

—— SNACKS ——

_____

WATER INTAKE ⛾⛾⛾⛾⛾⛾⛾⛾ ____ TOTAL OZ.

EXERCISE. . . . .

_____

_____

_____

_____

I HAD: ☐ AN AWESOME DAY! ☐ I CAN DO BETTER!

DATE _____

TODAY I ATE...

BREAKFAST

_____
_____
_____
_____

—— SNACKS ——

LUNCH

_____
_____
_____
_____

DINNER

_____
_____
_____
_____

WATER INTAKE ⬓⬓⬓⬓⬓⬓⬓⬓ _____ TOTAL OZ.

EXERCISE...

_____
_____
_____
_____

I HAD: ☐ AN AWESOME DAY! ☐ I CAN DO BETTER!

DATE _____

· · · · · · · **I SLEPT___ HOURS LAST NIGHT.** · · · · · · ·

TODAY I ATE...

BREAKFAST

_____

_____

_____

LUNCH

_____

_____

_____

DINNER

_____

_____

_____

_____

———— SNACKS ————

_____

WATER INTAKE ⛛⛛⛛⛛⛛⛛⛛ ____ TOTAL OZ.

EXERCISE...

_____

_____

_____

_____

I HAD: ☐ AN AWESOME DAY! ☐ I CAN DO BETTER!

DATE _____

TODAY I ATE...

BREAKFAST

_____
_____
_____
_____

LUNCH

_____
_____
_____
_____

DINNER

_____
_____
_____
_____

—— SNACKS ——

WATER INTAKE ⊔⊔⊔⊔⊔⊔⊔ _____ TOTAL OZ.

EXERCISE..

_____
_____
_____
_____

I HAD: ☐ AN AWESOME DAY! ☐ I CAN DO BETTER!

DATE _____

· · · · · · · · I SLEPT ___ HOURS LAST NIGHT. · · · · · ·

TODAY I ATE...

BREAKFAST

_____

_____

_____

_____

LUNCH

_____

_____

_____

_____

DINNER

_____

_____

_____

_____

— SNACKS —

_____

WATER INTAKE ⛶⛶⛶⛶⛶⛶⛶ ___ TOTAL OZ.

EXERCISE..

_____

_____

_____

_____

I HAD: ☐ AN AWESOME DAY! ☐ I CAN DO BETTER!

DATE _____

· · · · · · · **I SLEPT___ HOURS LAST NIGHT.** · · · · · ·

TODGA I ATE...

BREAKFAST

_____

_____

_____

_____

LUNCH

_____

_____

_____

_____

DINNER

_____

_____

_____

_____

— SNACKS —

_____

WATER INTAKE ▽▽▽▽▽▽▽ _____ TOTAL OZ.

EXERCISE..

_____

_____

_____

_____

_____

I HAD: ☐ AN AWESOME DAY! ☐ I CAN DO BETTER!

DATE _____

• • • • • • • I SLEPT ___ HOURS LAST NIGHT. • • • • • •

TODAY I ATE...

BREAKFAST

_____

_____

_____   — SNACKS —

_____

LUNCH

_____

_____

_____

_____

DINNER

_____

_____

_____   _____

_____

WATER INTAKE ⫿⫿⫿⫿⫿⫿⫿⫿ ___ TOTAL OZ

EXERCISE..

_____

_____

_____

_____

I HAD: ☐ AN AWESOME DAY! ☐ I CAN DO BETTER!

DATE _____

. . . . **I SLEPT___ HOURS LAST NIGHT.** . . . . . .

TODAY I ATE..

BREAKFAST

_____

_____

_____   — SNACKS —

_____

LUNCH

_____

_____

_____

_____

DINNER

_____

_____

_____   _____

_____

WATER INTAKE ⬛⬛⬛⬛⬛⬛⬛ ____ TOTAL OZ.

EXERCISE..

_____

_____

_____

I HAD: ☐ AN AWESOME DAY! ☐ I CAN DO BETTER!

DATE _____

I SLEPT ____ HOURS LAST NIGHT.

TODAY I ATE..

BREAKFAST
_____
_____
_____

LUNCH
_____
_____
_____

DINNER
_____
_____
_____

—— SNACKS ——

WATER INTAKE _____ TOTAL OZ.

EXERCISE..
_____
_____
_____
_____

I HAD: ☐ AN AWESOME DAY! ☐ I CAN DO BETTER!

DATE _____

I SLEPT ___ HOURS LAST NIGHT.

TODAY I ATE..

BREAKFAST

_____
_____
_____
_____

LUNCH

_____
_____
_____
_____

DINNER

_____
_____
_____
_____

—— SNACKS ——

_____

WATER INTAKE ⛉⛉⛉⛉⛉⛉⛉⛉ ____ TOTAL OZ

EXERCISE..

_____
_____
_____
_____

I HAD: ☐ AN AWESOME DAY! ☐ I CAN DO BETTER!

DATE _____

· · · · · · I SLEPT___ HOURS LAST NIGHT. · · · · · ·

TODAY I ATE..

BREAKFAST

_____

_____

_____

_____

LUNCH

_____

_____

_____

_____

DINNER

_____

_____

_____

_____

—— SNACKS ——

_____

WATER INTAKE ⛶⛶⛶⛶⛶⛶⛶ ___ TOTAL OZ.

EXERCISE..

_____

_____

_____

_____

I HAD: ☐ AN AWESOME DAY! ☐ I CAN DO BETTER!

DATE _____

TODAY I ATE . . . .

BREAKFAST

_____

_____

_____

_____

LUNCH

_____

_____

_____

_____

DINNER

_____

_____

_____

_____

——— SNACKS ———

_____

WATER INTAKE 🥤🥤🥤🥤🥤🥤🥤 _____ TOTAL OZ.

EXERCISE . . . .

_____

_____

_____

_____

I HAD: ☐ AN AWESOME DAY! ☐ I CAN DO BETTER!

DATE _____

I SLEPT ___ HOURS LAST NIGHT.

TODAY I ATE...

BREAKFAST

_____
_____
_____

LUNCH

_____
_____
_____
_____

DINNER

_____
_____
_____
_____

— SNACKS —

_____

WATER INTAKE ⛛⛛⛛⛛⛛⛛⛛ ___ TOTAL OZ.

EXERCISE...

_____
_____
_____
_____

I HAD: ☐ AN AWESOME DAY! ☐ I CAN DO BETTER!

DATE _____

· · · · · · · I SLEPT ___ HOURS LAST NIGHT. · · · · · ·

TODAY I ATE...

BREAKFAST

_____

_____ —— SNACKS ——

_____

_____

LUNCH

_____

_____

_____

_____

DINNER

_____

_____

_____ _____

WATER INTAKE ⛾⛾⛾⛾⛾⛾⛾ ____ TOTAL OZ.

EXERCISE...

_____

_____

_____

_____

I HAD: ☐ AN AWESOME DAY! ☐ I CAN DO BETTER!

DATE _____

TODAY I ATE..

BREAKFAST

_____
_____
_____
_____

LUNCH

_____
_____
_____
_____

DINNER

_____
_____
_____
_____

——— SNACKS ———

_____

WATER INTAKE ⎕⎕⎕⎕⎕⎕⎕ ___ TOTAL OZ.

EXERCISE..

_____
_____
_____
_____
_____

I HAD: ☐ AN AWESOME DAY! ☐ I CAN DO BETTER!

DATE _____

. . . . I SLEPT ___ HOURS LAST NIGHT. . . . . . .

TODAY I ATE. . . . .

BREAKFAST
_____
_____
_____
_____

LUNCH
_____
_____
_____
_____

DINNER
_____
_____
_____
_____

— SNACKS —

_____

WATER INTAKE ▽▽▽▽▽▽▽ ___ TOTAL OZ.

EXERCISE. . . . .
_____
_____
_____
_____

I HAD: ☐ AN AWESOME DAY! ☐ I CAN DO BETTER!

DATE _____

I SLEPT ____ HOURS LAST NIGHT.

TODAY I ATE..

BREAKFAST

_____
_____
_____
_____

LUNCH

_____
_____
_____
_____

DINNER

_____
_____
_____
_____

—— SNACKS ——

WATER INTAKE ⛶⛶⛶⛶⛶⛶⛶ ____ TOTAL OZ.

EXERCISE..

_____
_____
_____
_____

I HAD: ☐ AN AWESOME DAY! ☐ I CAN DO BETTER!

DATE _____

. . . . I SLEPT ___ HOURS LAST NIGHT. . . . . . .

TODAY I ATE . . . .

BREAKFAST

_____
_____
_____
_____

LUNCH

_____
_____
_____
_____

DINNER

_____
_____
_____

— SNACKS —

_____

WATER INTAKE ⬚⬚⬚⬚⬚⬚⬚ ___ TOTAL OZ.

EXERCISE . . . .

_____
_____
_____
_____

I HAD: ☐ AN AWESOME DAY! ☐ I CAN DO BETTER!

DATE _____

. . . . I SLEPT ___ HOURS LAST NIGHT. . . . . . .

TODAY I ATE...

BREAKFAST

_____
_____
_____
_____

LUNCH

_____
_____
_____
_____

DINNER

_____
_____
_____
_____

—— SNACKS ——

WATER INTAKE ⊔⊔⊔⊔⊔⊔⊔ ___ TOTAL OZ.

EXERCISE...

_____
_____
_____
_____

I HAD: ☐ AN AWESOME DAY! ☐ I CAN DO BETTER!

DATE _____

······· I SLEPT ___ HOURS LAST NIGHT. ·······

TODAY I ATE..

BREAKFAST

_____
_____
_____
_____

LUNCH

_____
_____
_____
_____

DINNER

_____
_____
_____
_____

—— SNACKS ——

_____

WATER INTAKE ⛆⛆⛆⛆⛆⛆⛆ ____ TOTAL OZ.

EXERCISE...

_____
_____
_____
_____

I HAD: ☐ AN AWESOME DAY! ☐ I CAN DO BETTER!

BIG THINGS HAPPEN ONE DAY AT A TIME

DATE _____

| · · · · · · · I SLEPT ___ HOURS LAST NIGHT. · · · · · · |

TODAY I ATE...

BREAKFAST

_____

_____

_____   — SNACKS —

_____

LUNCH

_____

_____

_____

_____

DINNER

_____

_____

_____   _____

_____

WATER INTAKE ▽▽▽▽▽▽▽ ___ TOTAL OZ

EXERCISE...

_____

_____

_____

_____

I HAD: ☐ AN AWESOME DAY! ☐ I CAN DO BETTER!

DATE _____

. . . . I SLEPT__ HOURS LAST NIGHT. . . . . . .

TODY I ATE......................................

BREAKFAST

_____
_____
_____
_____

—— SNACKS ——

LUNCH

_____
_____
_____
_____

DINNER

_____
_____
_____
_____

_____

WATER INTAKE ⊔⊔⊔⊔⊔⊔⊔ ___ TOTAL OZ.

XERCISE.....................................

_____
_____
_____
_____

I HAD: ☐ AN AWESOME DAY! ☐ I CAN DO BETTER!

DATE _____

· · · · · · · **I SLEPT___ HOURS LAST NIGHT.** · · · · · · ·

TODAY I ATE.......................................

BREAKFAST

_____
_____
_____
_____

LUNCH

_____
_____
_____
_____

DINNER

_____
_____
_____
_____

——— SNACKS ———

_____

WATER INTAKE ▽▽▽▽▽▽▽▽ ____ TOTAL OZ

EXERCISE...

_____
_____
_____
_____

I HAD: ☐ AN AWESOME DAY! ☐ I CAN DO BETTER!

DATE _____

. . . . I SLEPT___ HOURS LAST NIGHT. . . . . . .

TODAY I ATE. . . . .

BREAKFAST

_____
_____
_____
_____

LUNCH

_____
_____
_____
_____

DINNER

_____
_____
_____
_____

—— SNACKS ——

_____

WATER INTAKE   ▽▽▽▽▽▽▽ ___ TOTAL OZ.

EXERCISE. . . . .

_____
_____
_____
_____
_____

I HAD: ☐ AN AWESOME DAY! ☐ I CAN DO BETTER!

DATE _____

······· I SLEPT ___ HOURS LAST NIGHT. ·······

TODAY I ATE..

BREAKFAST

_____
_____
_____
_____

LUNCH

_____
_____
_____
_____

DINNER

_____
_____
_____
_____

—— SNACKS ——

_____

WATER INTAKE ▽▽▽▽▽▽▽▽ ___ TOTAL OZ

EXERCISE..

_____
_____
_____
_____

I HAD: ☐ AN AWESOME DAY! ☐ I CAN DO BETTER!

DATE _____

· · · · · · I SLEPT___ HOURS LAST NIGHT. · · · · · ·

ODAY I ATE. . . . .

BREAKFAST

_____

_____

_____   ── SNACKS ──

_____

LUNCH

_____

_____

_____

_____

DINNER

_____

_____

_____

_____

WATER INTAKE ▽▽▽▽▽▽▽ ____ TOTAL OZ.

XERCISE. . . . .

_____

_____

_____

_____

I HAD: ☐ AN AWESOME DAY! ☐ I CAN DO BETTER!

DATE _____

· · · · · · · I SLEPT ___ HOURS LAST NIGHT. · · · · · ·

TODAY I ATE..

BREAKFAST
_____
_____
_____
_____

——— SNACKS ———

LUNCH
_____
_____
_____
_____

DINNER
_____
_____
_____
_____

_____

WATER INTAKE ⛶⛶⛶⛶⛶⛶⛶⛶ ___ TOTAL OZ.

EXERCISE..
_____
_____
_____
_____

I HAD: ☐ AN AWESOME DAY! ☐ I CAN DO BETTER!

DATE _____

I SLEPT ____ HOURS LAST NIGHT. . . . . . .

TODAY I ATE . . . .

BREAKFAST

_____

_____

_____

LUNCH

_____

_____

_____

DINNER

_____

_____

_____

_____

—— SNACKS ——

WATER INTAKE ⟄⟄⟄⟄⟄⟄⟄ ____ TOTAL OZ.

EXERCISE . . . .

_____

_____

_____

_____

I HAD: ☐ AN AWESOME DAY! ☐ I CAN DO BETTER!

DATE _____

· · · · · · · **I SLEPT** ___ **HOURS LAST NIGHT.** · · · · · ·

TODAY I ATE......................................

BREAKFAST

_____
_____
_____
_____

LUNCH

_____
_____
_____
_____

DINNER

_____
_____
_____
_____

—— SNACKS ——

_____

WATER INTAKE ▽▽▽▽▽▽▽▽ ___ TOTAL OZ.

EXERCISE......................................

_____
_____
_____
_____

I HAD: ☐ AN AWESOME DAY! ☐ I CAN DO BETTER!

DATE _____

· · · · · · **I SLEPT___ HOURS LAST NIGHT.** · · · · · ·

TODAY I ATE...

BREAKFAST

_____
_____
_____
_____

LUNCH

_____
_____
_____
_____

DINNER

_____
_____
_____
_____

—— SNACKS ——

_____

WATER INTAKE ▽▽▽▽▽▽▽ ___ TOTAL OZ.

XERCISE...

_____
_____
_____
_____

I HAD: ☐ AN AWESOME DAY! ☐ I CAN DO BETTER!

DATE _____

· · · · · · · · **I SLEPT___ HOURS LAST NIGHT.** · · · · · ·

TODAY I ATE . . . .

BREAKFAST
_____
_____
_____
_____

LUNCH
_____
_____
_____
_____

DINNER
_____
_____
_____
_____

—— SNACKS ——

_____

WATER INTAKE ⛶⛶⛶⛶⛶⛶⛶⛶ ___ TOTAL OZ.

EXERCISE . . . .

_____
_____
_____
_____

I HAD: ☐ AN AWESOME DAY! ☐ I CAN DO BETTER!

DATE _____

• • • • • • • I SLEPT ___ HOURS LAST NIGHT. • • • • • •

TODAY I ATE...

BREAKFAST

_____
_____
_____
_____

LUNCH

_____
_____
_____
_____

DINNER

_____
_____
_____
_____

——— SNACKS ———

_____

WATER INTAKE ⛉⛉⛉⛉⛉⛉⛉ ___ TOTAL OZ.

EXERCISE...

_____
_____
_____
_____

I HAD: ☐ AN AWESOME DAY! ☐ I CAN DO BETTER!

DATE _____

· · · · · · · **I SLEPT___ HOURS LAST NIGHT.** · · · · · ·

TODAY I ATE..

BREAKFAST
_____
_____
_____
_____

LUNCH
_____
_____
_____
_____

DINNER
_____
_____
_____
_____

——— SNACKS ———
_____

WATER INTAKE ▽▽▽▽▽▽▽ ___ TOTAL OZ

EXERCISE...
_____
_____
_____
_____

I HAD: ☐ AN AWESOME DAY! ☐ I CAN DO BETTER!

DATE _____

• • • • • • • I SLEPT ___ HOURS LAST NIGHT. • • • • • • •

TODAY I ATE . . . .

BREAKFAST

_____

_____

_____

_____

LUNCH

_____

_____

_____

DINNER

_____

_____

_____

— SNACKS —

_____

WATER INTAKE ⧖⧖⧖⧖⧖⧖⧖ ___ TOTAL OZ

EXERCISE . . . .

_____

_____

_____

_____

I HAD: ☐ AN AWESOME DAY! ☐ I CAN DO BETTER!

DATE _____

. . . . . . I SLEPT ___ HOURS LAST NIGHT. . . . . . .

TODAY I ATE. . . . .

BREAKFAST

_____

_____

_____   — SNACKS —

_____

LUNCH

_____

_____

_____

_____

DINNER

_____

_____

_____

_____

WATER INTAKE ⛶⛶⛶⛶⛶⛶⛶⛶ _____ TOTAL OZ.

EXERCISE. . . . .

_____

_____

_____

_____

_____

I HAD: ☐ AN AWESOME DAY! ☐ I CAN DO BETTER!

DATE _____

· · · · · · · I SLEPT___ HOURS LAST NIGHT. · · · · · ·

TODAY I ATE...

BREAKFAST

_____

_____

_____

LUNCH

_____

_____

_____

DINNER

_____

_____

_____

—— SNACKS ——

_____

WATER INTAKE ▽▽▽▽▽▽▽ ___ TOTAL OZ

EXERCISE..

_____

_____

_____

_____

I HAD: ☐ AN AWESOME DAY! ☐ I CAN DO BETTER!

DATE _____

. . . . **I SLEPT ___ HOURS LAST NIGHT.** . . . . . .

TODAY I ATE..

BREAKFAST

_____
_____
_____
_____

LUNCH

_____
_____
_____

DINNER

_____
_____
_____

—— SNACKS ——

WATER INTAKE ⊓⊓⊓⊓⊓⊓⊓ ___ TOTAL OZ.

XERCISE..

_____
_____
_____
_____

I HAD: ☐ AN AWESOME DAY! ☐ I CAN DO BETTER!

DATE _____

TODAY I ATE..

BREAKFAST
_____
_____
_____
_____

LUNCH
_____
_____
_____

DINNER
_____
_____
_____

— SNACKS —

_____

WATER INTAKE ⊔⊔⊔⊔⊔⊔⊔ ____ TOTAL OZ

EXERCISE..
_____
_____
_____
_____

I HAD: ☐ AN AWESOME DAY! ☐ I CAN DO BETTER!

DATE _____

. . . . **I SLEPT___ HOURS LAST NIGHT.** . . . . . .

TODY I ATE...

BREAKFAST

_____
_____
_____
_____

LUNCH

_____
_____
_____
_____

DINNER

_____
_____
_____
_____

┌─────────────┐
│ — SNACKS — │
│   │
│   │
│   │
│   │
│   │
│   │
│ _____ │
└─────────────┘

WATER INTAKE ▽▽▽▽▽▽▽ ___ TOTAL OZ.

XERCISE..

_____
_____
_____
_____

I HAD: ☐ AN AWESOME DAY! ☐ I CAN DO BETTER!

DATE _____

· · · · · · · I SLEPT ___ HOURS LAST NIGHT. · · · · · ·

TODAY I ATE...

BREAKFAST

_____
_____
_____   ─── SNACKS ───
_____

LUNCH

_____
_____
_____
_____

DINNER

_____
_____
_____   _____
_____

WATER INTAKE ▽▽▽▽▽▽▽ ___ TOTAL OZ.

EXERCISE..

_____
_____
_____
_____

I HAD: ☐ AN AWESOME DAY! ☐ I CAN DO BETTER!

DATE _____

· · · · · · I SLEPT ___ HOURS LAST NIGHT. · · · · · ·

TODAY I ATE...

BREAKFAST

_____
_____
_____
_____

LUNCH

_____
_____
_____
_____

DINNER

_____
_____
_____
_____

—— SNACKS ——

_____

WATER INTAKE ⬜⬜⬜⬜⬜⬜⬜ ___ TOTAL OZ.

XERCISE...

_____
_____
_____
_____
_____

I HAD: ⬜ AN AWESOME DAY! ⬜ I CAN DO BETTER!

DATE _____

. . . . **I SLEPT ___ HOURS LAST NIGHT.** . . . .

TODY I ATE..

BREAKFAST

_____

_____

_____   ── SNACKS ──

_____

LUNCH

_____

_____

_____

DINNER

_____

_____

_____

WATER INTAKE ▽▽▽▽▽▽▽ ___ TOTAL OZ.

EXERCISE...

_____

_____

_____

_____

I HAD: ☐ AN AWESOME DAY! ☐ I CAN DO BETTER!

DATE _____

. . . . **I SLEPT___ HOURS LAST NIGHT.** . . . . . .

TODAY I ATE..

BREAKFAST

_____
_____
_____
_____

LUNCH

_____
_____
_____
_____

DINNER

_____
_____
_____
_____

—— SNACKS ——

WATER INTAKE ▽▽▽▽▽▽▽ ___ TOTAL OZ.

XERCISE...

_____
_____
_____
_____
_____

I HAD: ☐ AN AWESOME DAY! ☐ I CAN DO BETTER!

DATE _____

· · · · · · · **I SLEPT ___ HOURS LAST NIGHT.** · · · · · ·

TODAY I ATE...

BREAKFAST

_____

_____

_____   — SNACKS —

_____

LUNCH

_____

_____

_____

_____

DINNER

_____

_____

_____   _____

_____

WATER INTAKE ▽▽▽▽▽▽▽ ___ TOTAL OZ

EXERCISE...

_____

_____

_____

_____

I HAD: ☐ AN AWESOME DAY! ☐ I CAN DO BETTER!

DATE _____

• • • • • • • I SLEPT___ HOURS LAST NIGHT. • • • • • •

TODAY I ATE...

BREAKFAST

_____
_____
_____
_____

┌─────────────────┐
│ ——— SNACKS ——— │

LUNCH

_____
_____
_____
_____

DINNER

_____
_____
_____
_____
                              └─────────────────┘

WATER INTAKE ▽▽▽▽▽▽▽ ___ TOTAL OZ.

EXERCISE...

_____
_____
_____
_____

I HAD: ☐ AN AWESOME DAY! ☐ I CAN DO BETTER!

DATE _____

I SLEPT ___ HOURS LAST NIGHT.

TODAY I ATE...

BREAKFAST
_____
_____
_____
_____

LUNCH
_____
_____
_____
_____

DINNER
_____
_____
_____

——— SNACKS ———
_____

WATER INTAKE ⛛⛛⛛⛛⛛⛛⛛⛛ ——— TOTAL OZ.

EXERCISE...
_____
_____
_____
_____

I HAD: ☐ AN AWESOME DAY! ☐ I CAN DO BETTER!

GOOD THINGS COME TO THOSE WHO SWEAT

DATE _____

. . . . I SLEPT ___ HOURS LAST NIGHT. . . . .

TODAY I ATE...

BREAKFAST

_____

_____

_____

_____

LUNCH

_____

_____

_____

_____

DINNER

_____

_____

_____

_____

—— SNACKS ——

_____

WATER INTAKE ⬚⬚⬚⬚⬚⬚⬚⬚ ___ TOTAL OZ.

EXERCISE...

_____

_____

_____

_____

I HAD: ☐ AN AWESOME DAY! ☐ I CAN DO BETTER!

DATE _____

. . . . **I SLEPT___ HOURS LAST NIGHT.** . . . . . .

TODAY I ATE...

BREAKFAST

_____
_____
_____   ┌─────────────────┐
_____   │   — SNACKS —   │
                                          │   │
LUNCH   │   │
                                          │   │
_____   │   │
_____   │   │
_____   │   │
_____   │   │
                                          │   │
DINNER   │   │
                                          │   │
_____   │   │
_____   │   │
_____   │ _____ │
                                          └─────────────────┘

WATER INTAKE ⊔⊔⊔⊔⊔⊔⊔ ____ TOTAL OZ.

EXERCISE...

_____
_____
_____
_____

I HAD: ☐ AN AWESOME DAY! ☐ I CAN DO BETTER!

DATE _____

· · · · · · · I SLEPT ___ HOURS LAST NIGHT. · · · · · · ·

TODAY I ATE..

BREAKFAST

_____

_____

_____

_____

LUNCH

_____

_____

_____

_____

DINNER

_____

_____

_____

_____

—— SNACKS ——

_____

WATER INTAKE ▽▽▽▽▽▽▽▽ ___ TOTAL OZ

EXERCISE...

_____

_____

_____

_____

I HAD: ☐ AN AWESOME DAY! ☐ I CAN DO BETTER!

DATE _____

• • • • • • **I SLEPT___ HOURS LAST NIGHT.** • • • • • •

TODAY I ATE..

BREAKFAST

_____

_____

_____

_____

LUNCH

_____

_____

_____

_____

DINNER

_____

_____

_____

_____

—— SNACKS ——

_____

WATER INTAKE ▽▽▽▽▽▽▽ ___ TOTAL OZ.

EXERCISE..

_____

_____

_____

_____

I HAD: ☐ AN AWESOME DAY! ☐ I CAN DO BETTER!

DATE _____

. . . . **I SLEPT ___ HOURS LAST NIGHT.** . . . . .

TODODAY I ATE...

BREAKFAST

_____
_____
_____   ⎯ SNACKS ⎯
_____

LUNCH

_____
_____
_____
_____

DINNER

_____
_____
_____
_____   _____

WATER INTAKE ▽▽▽▽▽▽▽▽ _____ TOTAL OZ

EXERCISE..

_____
_____
_____
_____

I HAD: ☐ AN AWESOME DAY! ☐ I CAN DO BETTER!

DATE _____

· · · · · · · I SLEPT___ HOURS LAST NIGHT. · · · · · · ·

TODY I ATE..

BREAKFAST

_____
_____
_____
_____

LUNCH

_____
_____
_____
_____

DINNER

_____
_____
_____
_____

— SNACKS —

WATER INTAKE ▽▽▽▽▽▽▽ ___ TOTAL OZ.

XERCISE...

_____
_____
_____
_____
_____

I HAD: ☐ AN AWESOME DAY! ☐ I CAN DO BETTER!

DATE _____

| . . . . **I SLEPT ___ HOURS LAST NIGHT.** . . . . |

TODAY I ATE..

BREAKFAST

_____

_____

_____   ——— SNACKS ———

_____

LUNCH

_____

_____

_____

_____

DINNER

_____

_____

_____   _____

_____

WATER INTAKE ⛛⛛⛛⛛⛛⛛⛛⛛ _____ TOTAL OZ

EXERCISE...

_____

_____

_____

_____

I HAD: ☐ AN AWESOME DAY! ☐ I CAN DO BETTER!

DATE _____

· · · · · · I SLEPT__ HOURS LAST NIGHT. · · · · · ·

TODAY I ATE..

BREAKFAST

_____

_____

_____

LUNCH

_____

_____

_____

DINNER

_____

_____

_____

—— SNACKS ——

WATER INTAKE ____ TOTAL OZ.

EXERCISE...

_____

_____

_____

_____

I HAD: ☐ AN AWESOME DAY! ☐ I CAN DO BETTER!

DATE _____

· · · · · · · **I SLEPT___ HOURS LAST NIGHT.** · · · · · ·

TODAY I ATE...

BREAKFAST

_____

_____

_____

LUNCH

_____

_____

_____

DINNER

_____

_____

_____

——— SNACKS ———

_____

WATER INTAKE ▯▯▯▯▯▯▯ ___ TOTAL OZ.

EXERCISE..

_____

_____

_____

_____

I HAD: ☐ AN AWESOME DAY! ☐ I CAN DO BETTER!

DATE _____

. . . . I SLEPT____ HOURS LAST NIGHT. . . . . . .

TODAY I ATE. . . . .

BREAKFAST

_____

_____

_____   ———— SNACKS ————

_____

LUNCH

_____

_____

_____

_____

DINNER

_____

_____

_____

_____

WATER INTAKE ⊔⊔⊔⊔⊔⊔⊔⊔ ———— TOTAL OZ.

EXERCISE. . . . .

_____

_____

_____

_____

I HAD: ☐ AN AWESOME DAY! ☐ I CAN DO BETTER!

DATE _____

· · · · · · · I SLEPT ___ HOURS LAST NIGHT. · · · · · ·

TODAY I ATE...

BREAKFAST

_____
_____
_____
_____

LUNCH

_____
_____
_____
_____

DINNER

_____
_____
_____
_____

—— SNACKS ——

WATER INTAKE ▽▽▽▽▽▽▽ ___ TOTAL OZ

EXERCISE...

_____
_____
_____
_____

I HAD: ☐ AN AWESOME DAY! ☐ I CAN DO BETTER!

DATE _____

I SLEPT ____ HOURS LAST NIGHT.

TODAY I ATE...

BREAKFAST

_____
_____
_____
_____

LUNCH

_____
_____
_____
_____

DINNER

_____
_____
_____

——— SNACKS ———

WATER INTAKE ⊔⊔⊔⊔⊔⊔⊔ ____ TOTAL OZ.

XERCISE...

_____
_____
_____
_____

I HAD: ☐ AN AWESOME DAY! ☐ I CAN DO BETTER!

PROGRESS CHECK POINT

STATS

WEIGHT ....

CHEST ....

WAIST ....

HIPS ....

THIGH ....

CALF ....

OVERALL FEELINGS TOWARDS:

NUTRITION

TERRIBLE   NOT GOOD   I'M OKAY   GRRREAT   FOOD NINJA

EXERCISE

TERRIBLE   NOT GOOD   I'M OKAY   GRRREAT   EXERCISE NINJA

R·E·M·E·M·B·E·R

Progress > Perfection

YOU ARE AWESOME!

27939170R00057

Made in the USA
Lexington, KY
08 January 2019